SWEAR
Word
YOU CAN
BE
HAPPY
THIS COLORING BOOK BELONGS TO:

THANK YOU FOR BUYING MY COLORING BOOK.

Get ready to entertain your creative brain with **40 hilarious swear word coloring designs.**

There's so much variety to make you smile. You'll find fantastic Flowers, whimsical, typography, fabulous flowers and cool patterns. All served up with funny swear words that will help you laugh and bitchslap your stress!

Before you start coloring, here's a little tip: Amazon's choice of printing paper is primarily designed for colored pencils. If you prefer to use markers, I would recommend placing a piece of paper behind the page you are coloring to avoid bleed-through.

Laugh, Color and Relax!

Happy coloring!

If you enjoyed my Coloring Book please consider leaving a review. It means the world to me.

Thank you!

COLOR TESTING PAGE

FUCK FUCK FUCK

FUCK FUCK FUCK

FUCK FUCK FUCK

FUCK FUCK FUCK

FUCK FUCK FUCK

FUCK FUCK FUCK

Don't
Fucking
Give up

FUCK
AROUND
&
FIND
OUT

Shit On The Haters

Own
Your
Fucking
Power

Take No Shit From Anyone

Build
Your
Empire
Bitch

Build
Your
Empire
Bitch

I
Am
A
Fucking
Warrior

FUCK
WHAT
THEY
THINK

Bitch
DON'T
KILL
MY
Vibe

Make
LIFE
YOUR
Bitch

Crush
Those
FUCKING
Goals

UNFUCK
YOUR
Brain

Calm The Fuck Down

Son
of a
Bitch

Kiss My Ass

I Don't
GIVE A
Shit

NO ONE
fucking
CARES

I Will
Manifest That
Shit

Shit
Thinks
Take
Time

Fresh
Out of
Fuck

FUCK
it all

COCK
SUCKER

Fuck
Reality

TAKING
The
Piss

Fuck
Off

Fair Suck Of The Sav

DOG'S BOLLOCKS

BEEF
Curtains

FUCK
You

PISS
OFF

Dick
HEAD

Damn You

BOLLOCKS

BLOODY
Hell

Shit

Asshole

Bastard

BITCH

CUNT
FUN